Week-by-Week Phonics Packets

30 Independent Practice Packets That Help Children Learn Key Phonics Skills and Set the Stage for Reading Success

Joan Novelli & Holly Grundon

New York • Toronto • London • Auckland • Sydney
Mexico City • New Delhi • Hong Kong • Buenos Aires

Teaching *Resources*

Special thanks to Carlyle Grundon
for inspiring and helping with "Big Cheek Chipmunk."

"Fox and Frog" is adapted from "Log Hop" from *File-Folder Pocket Charts: Phonics Poems* by Kathleen Hollenbeck (Scholastic, 2010). Text copyright © 2010 by Kathleen Hollenbeck. Used by permission of the author.

"The Great Green Bean," "A Grouchy Day," "Have You Ever?," "Letter Rhymes,"
"More Than One," "What Can a Dog Do?," and "Where Is Short *u*?" copyright © 2010 by Joan Novelli.

Cover design: Holly Grundon
Interior design: On the Ball Productions
Interior illustrations: Maxie Chambliss, Kate Flanagan, James Graham Hale, Bari Weissman

ISBN-13: 978-0-545-22304-1
ISBN 10: 0-545-22304-0

Published by Scholastic Inc.
All rights reserved.
Printed in the U.S.A.

22 23 24   40   24 23 22 21

Contents

Phonics Packets

About This Book

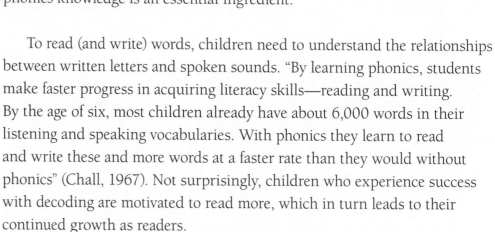

Young children possess an instinctive drive to "do it all by myself." They delight in each independent step they take—choosing their own clothes, riding a bike, tying their shoes. Reading is one of those "I can do it all by myself" milestones, and the motivation children naturally have to read is an important factor in their success. But cracking the code of reading requires much more, and as research consistently shows, phonics knowledge is an essential ingredient.

To read (and write) words, children need to understand the relationships between written letters and spoken sounds. "By learning phonics, students make faster progress in acquiring literacy skills—reading and writing. By the age of six, most children already have about 6,000 words in their listening and speaking vocabularies. With phonics they learn to read and write these and more words at a faster rate than they would without phonics" (Chall, 1967). Not surprisingly, children who experience success with decoding are motivated to read more, which in turn leads to their continued growth as readers.

Learning to read is a lot like so many other things children want to be able to do on their own—it requires both instruction and practice. To promote reading success, *Week-by-Week Phonics Packets* features hundreds of engaging activities that systematically support children's acquisition of word-recognition skills and strategies. When used in conjunction with direct instruction as part of a balanced literacy program, these phonics packets offer an appealing approach to practice that helps children achieve the real goal: ". . . to recognize words, quickly and automatically, so that they can turn their attention to comprehension of text" (Stahl, 1992). It's a transformational time in a child's life when this begins to happen, and the confidence that comes with that "I can do it all by myself" moment is a lasting asset.

Teaching Tip

The phonics packets in this book focus on those sound-spelling relationships that children can most readily apply in their reading and writing. For example, packets on vowel sounds include both *ay* as in *day* (page 66) and *oo* as in *moon* (page 81). However, some spelling patterns, such as the long *i* made by the vowel digraph *ey* in *geyser*, are of less use to early readers and for this reason are not covered in the practice pages.

4

Teaching With the Phonics Packets

Week-by-Week Phonics Packets is designed for flexible use—both in terms of instructional goals and grouping options. And with five pages of activities in each packet, children may complete as much or as little as is determined to be appropriate at a pace that meets each learner's needs. Suggestions for using the phonics packets to meet the needs of your young learners follow.

✱ **Independent or Partner Work:** The formatted structure of the packets makes them ideal for children to complete on their own or with a partner. Assign the packets following whole-class instruction to provide practice.

✱ **Small-Group Work:** Use the packets with groups of children to address a common need. Children will benefit from the ideas they share with one another about their phonics knowledge and how to approach various activities.

✱ **Homework:** Send home the phonics packets to be completed with family members. Include a note explaining what children are learning in class, and the benefits of practicing at home.

Phonics-Packet Format

Each packet in *Week-by-Week Phonics Packets* is organized around a structured set of activities designed to motivate independent learning and support success. Though children will encounter a different skill with each packet, they will soon become familiar with the format, which will allow them to focus their energies on the learning at hand, develop confidence in their abilities, and take important steps in acquiring the skills they need to become fluent readers. Following is an overview of the basic format.

Page 1: Each phonics packet begins with an introduction to the new skill. Letters, pictures, and words engage children in thinking about what they already know and previewing the skills they will practice. A checklist on this page makes it easy for children to keep track of their progress as they complete each packet.

Page 2: A themed activity provides a playful approach to practice. For example, "Kittens and Mittens" (page 17), inspired by the favorite nursery rhyme ("Three Little Kittens"), invites children to explore rhyming words.

Page 3: Short activities provide practice in easy-to-manage chunks and accessible formats.

Page 4: Riddles, fill-in rhymes and stories, and sentence completions invite children to apply skills to connected text.

Page 5 (Review): Word hunts, word webs ("Word Tree"), and multiple-choice-format activities further reinforce skills. A self-assessment on this page invites children to evaluate their work and set goals for continued learning.

Each Packet Includes:

PAGE 1

PAGE 2

PAGE 3

PAGE 4

PAGE 5 (Review)

Activity Formats

Following is an overview of the basic activity formats children will encounter as they complete the phonics packets. When assigning a new phonics packet, take time to review the activities on each page. (See Mini-Lesson, page 7.) Invite children to share what they already know about particular activities, and provide clarification as needed. Model completing each type of activity children will finish in a given packet (as in the Mini-Lesson) before having children complete activities on their own.

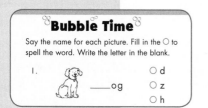

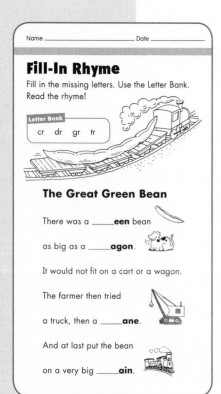

Bubble Time: This setup introduces a multiple-choice format.

Buddy Words: These playful buddies invite children to work with words in a variety of ways, for example, combining a consonant with a phonogram (onset, rime) to build a word.

Challenge Word: Children say the name for a picture, then apply their knowledge of sound-spelling relationships to fill in missing letters and spell a tricky word—a rewarding experience that builds confidence and motivates learning.

Fill-In Story (Fill-In Rhyme): These cloze-format activities invite children to use words in context and practice spelling words they are learning.

How Did You Do? A simple self-assessment lets children evaluate their work and set learning goals.

Make New Words: Children use what they know about sounds and letters to spell words.

Missing Letters: A Letter Bank contains the missing letters children need to complete words.

Puzzle Play: Children match puzzle pieces to practice skills.

Riddle Time (and What Am I?): Children practice reading words in context to fill in missing words and solve riddles.

Shape Match: Children attend to letter features as they practice reading and writing words in a puzzle format.

Spelling Scramble: Children use what they are learning about spelling patterns to rearrange letters and spell words. Picture clues provide support.

Thumbs Up! Children analyze words to decide if they meet the identified sound-spelling pattern, then indicate their answer by coloring in the "thumbs up" or "thumbs down" sign.

Two-Way Words: These little puzzles challenge children to make connections among words.

What Doesn't Belong? Children use what they know to identify words in a group that do not share a common characteristic (such as the beginning sound).

What's the Word? This format challenges children to use clues to figure out words.

Word Hunt: Children read and write words as they complete a word search.

Word Sort (also Letter Sort): Children sort letters and words according to various rules.

Words to Know: This list introduces words that represent the target skill. Pictures provide support for young readers.

Word Tree: As a review, children think of and write words they know to complete a word-web graphic organizer.

Mini-Lesson: Introducing the Phonics Packets

Use the following mini-lesson as a guide to introduce the phonics packets and engage children in thinking about what they know and making connections.

1 Begin by establishing a purpose for completing the activities. For example, if you are teaching with the Short *i* packet (page 41), remind children what they have already learned about the letter *i*. Explain that practicing what they have learned is an important step in learning to read and write new words with the short *i*.

2 After reviewing the target skill, invite children to volunteer words (including their names) that have that sound—for example, *William*, *Lily*, and *six* all share the short-*i* sound-spelling pattern.

3 Write the words on the board or chart paper. Read the words together, running your finger under the letters to reinforce sound-spelling relationships.

4 Take a few minutes to "read around the room" together, looking for additional examples of words on wall charts and other environmental print.

5 Display each page of the packet (one at a time) and model the process for completing the activities. Think aloud about following directions, making connections to what you already know, problem solving, and checking your work.

6 Guide children in setting individual goals for completing the packet over a period of time, for example, one week.

Week-by-Week Phonics Packets © 2010 by Joan Novelli and Holly Grundon. Scholastic Teaching Resources

---

Teaching Tip

When using any of the packets, it's always a good idea to begin with what children know best—their names, the names of important people in their lives, and other words with special significance. For example, when introducing the packet on short *a* (page 31), encourage children to identify classmates' names with this vowel sound (such as *Max* and *Jack*). Preparing for a packet on compound words (page 151)? *Playground* is a familiar word that will motivate children to learn more.

Point out the different sounds letters stand for to help children develop strategies they can apply to new words. For example, when teaching the CVCe spelling pattern for words with *u* (page 61), explain that the vowel sound children hear in *cube* is called the long-*u* sound. Point out that words such as *flute* are also considered long *u*, but the sound of *u* in this case has the /$\overline{oo}$/ sound. Similarly, as children explore the long-*e* spelling pattern *ea* (page 71), you might take time to introduce other sounds these letters stand for, including the short *e* in *bread* and *thread*.

Suggestions for Differentiated Learning

For children who are not ready to complete the entire packet or need more guidance, or for children who are ready to go further, try the following suggestions.

To Simplify the Packet

* Use sticky notes to identify those activities you wish children to complete.

* Pair children with students who are able to work more independently and offer assistance as needed.

To Provide a Challenge

* Using one of the activities from their packet as a model, have children create a new activity (based on the same phonics skill). Use the new activities as a quick review of previously taught/practiced skills before teaching a new skill or introducing a new packet.

* Provide children with writing opportunities that incorporate target words from the packet. Stories, poems, and riddles are all free-writing options. Encourage a playful approach to promote enjoyment of both the writing process and language exploration.

Extending Student Learning

Use the following ideas with any of the phonics packets to provide additional practice and extend learning.

Print Awareness: As children complete phonics packets, take time to reinforce concepts of print.

* Invite children to point out upper- and lowercase letter pairs on a page, as well as different shapes and sizes of letters.

* Have children track words they read from left to right.

* Discuss how spaces between words in a group (such as in activity directions or other sentences) help readers make sense of text.

* Have children notice the way some pictures and words in their packets go together. Guide children to recognize that they can use the pictures in books to help read and understand the words.

* Beginning with the words *Name* and *Date* on each page, use the packets to reinforce that words on a page correspond to speech.

Fluency Word Lists: Have children copy words from each packet in list form and practice reading them with a partner and independently. Children can add to the list with each packet they complete, revisiting words from previous packets to continue to build word recognition and fluency while also practicing new words.

Word Cut-Ups: Write words that contain the target skill on sentence strips, then cut apart the strip word by word. Cut apart each word (for example, letter by letter or by onset-rime or other word parts) and have children reassemble the words like puzzles.

Tell Me a Story: Have children make up stories using target words from the phonics packets. They can share their stories with you or a classmate to reinforce learning and strengthen oral language skills.

Word Sorts: Write words that represent target skills from each lesson on index cards (one word per card) and have children use them for words sorts. Examples follow.

* Sort words into groups according to target sound-spelling patterns, such as short *a* and short *e*.

* Sort words by number of letters.

* Sort words by number of syllables.

* Sort words into three groups as follows: Long-Vowel Sound, Short-Vowel Sound, and Other.

* Sort words according to "Words I Can Read" and "Words I Don't Know Yet."

Pocket Chart Practice: With children, come up with sentences that include target words from a packet and write them on sentence strips. Leave a blank (sized to fit the word) for each target word. Write target words on a sentence strip and cut apart to make word cards. Place the sentences in a pocket chart and the word cards at the bottom (or side). Let children work with a partner to place the word cards in the matching sentences and read them. To use for practice with a small group, place the sentence strips in the pocket chart and give each child a word card. Read the sentences one at a time and have the child with the missing word place it in the blank. Reread each complete sentence together. To provide additional support for either version, color-code the sentence strips and word cards.

Magnetic Words: Provide a bucket of magnetic letter tiles and a magnetic whiteboard (or other surface). Let children use the letters to spell words from their packets. Challenge them to spell new words that have the same spelling patterns.

Week-by-Week Phonics Packets © 2010 by Joan Novelli and Holly Grundon. Scholastic Teaching Resources

> ## Teaching Tip
>
> To encourage self-checking, create an answer key for each packet, completing the activities on each page in a color (such as blue) that stands out from the printed text and is easy for children to read. Use a highlighter to mark words in word searches and other activities that require students to locate words or letters in the text.

Connections to the Standards

The phonics packets in this book are designed to support you in meeting the following standards as outlined by Mid-continent Research for Education and Learning (McREL), an organization that collects and synthesizes national and state curriculum standards—and proposes what teachers should provide for their students to become proficient in language arts, among other curriculum areas.

Reading	Writing
✳ Knows that print and written symbols convey meaning and represent spoken language	**✳** Knows that writing, including pictures, letters, and words, communicates meaning and information
✳ Knows letters of the alphabet	**✳** Uses conventions of print in writing (e.g., forms letters in print, uses upper- and lowercase letters of the alphabet, spaces words and sentences, writes from left to right)
✳ Knows familiar words in print	
✳ Uses emergent reading skills	
✳ Uses visual and verbal cues to comprehend new words	**✳** Uses knowledge of letters to write or copy familiar words
✳ Uses basic elements of phonetic analysis	**✳** Uses phonic knowledge and conventions of spelling in writing (e.g., spells high-frequency, commonly misspelled words from appropriate grade-level list; spells phonetically regular words; uses letter-sound relationships; spells basic short-vowel, long-vowel, *r*-controlled, and consonant-blend patterns)
✳ Uses basic elements of structural analysis	
✳ Understands level-appropriate sight words and vocabulary	
✳ Uses self-correction strategies	

Source: *Content Knowledge: A Compendium of Standards and Benchmarks for K–12 Education* (4th ed.). Mid-continent Research for Education and Learning, 2004 (http://www.mcrel.org/standards–benchmarks).

References and Resources

Blevins, W. (2006). *Phonics from A to Z: A practical guide* (2nd ed.). New York: Scholastic.

Burns, M. S., Griffin, P., & Snow, C. E. (Eds.). (1999). *Starting out right: A guide to promoting children's reading success.* Washington, DC: The National Academy Press.

Chall, J. S. (1967). *Learning to read: The great debate.* New York: McGraw-Hill.

National Reading Panel. (2002). *Teaching children to read.* Washington, DC: Division of Research and Policy, International Reading Association.

Stahl, S. A. (1992). Saying the 'p' word: Nine guidelines for exemplary phonics instruction. *The Reading Teacher, 45*(8), 618–625.

Name _____ Date _____

ABC Path

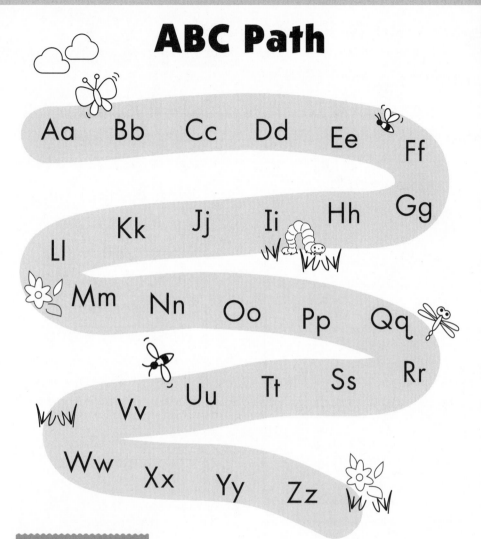

Letter Sort

Look at the letters on the ABC Path.
Fill in the boxes.

Letters in My First Name	5 Letters Not in My First Name

My Checklist

✔ **Check each activity when you complete it.**

Page 1

_____ ABC Path

_____ Letter Sort

Page 2

_____ Letter Friends

_____ What Doesn't Belong?

Page 3

_____ Puzzle Play

_____ Missing Letters

_____ Shape Match

Page 4

_____ Fill-In Rhyme

_____ Buddy Letters

_____ What Am I?

Page 5

_____ Review

Name _____ Date _____

Letter Friends

Help these letters find their friends.
Draw a line to match each uppercase
letter with its lowercase letter.

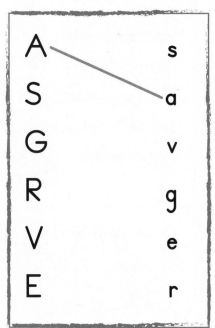

A	s
S	a
G	v
R	g
V	e
E	r

B	k
F	b
K	f
U	o
O	n
N	u

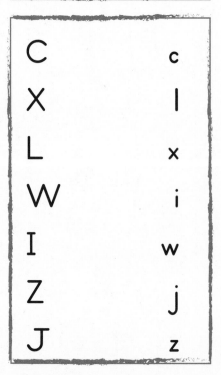

C	c
X	l
L	x
W	i
I	w
Z	j
J	z

D	y
M	d
Y	m
P	t
Q	p
T	q
H	h

What Doesn't Belong?

Find the matching
uppercase and
lowercase letters
in each row. ✗
the letter that
does not belong.

i	I	W
r	q	Q
D	L	d
H	h	n
p	f	P
S	B	b

Name _____ Date _____

Puzzle Play

Draw a line to match look-alike letters.

1.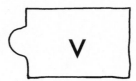

2.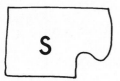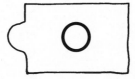

3.

4.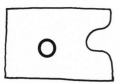

Shape Match

Look at the letters.
Find the matching shape.
Fill in the letters.

Cc   Jj
   Kk

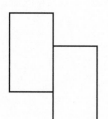   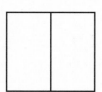   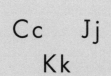 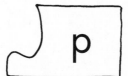

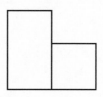

Missing Letters

Say the name
for each picture.
Write the letter
that matches
the beginning
sound. Use the
Letter Bank.

Letter Bank

Ff Ll Mm Nn Rr

Mm

_____

_____

_____

_____

Fill-In Rhyme

Fill in the letters to complete the rhyme.
Use the Letter Bank.

Letter Bank

C L O Q R

Letter Rhymes

The letter _____ rhymes with .

What rhymes with ?

The letter _____ !

_____ rhymes with 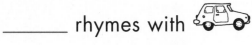

and _____ with  .

The rhyme for _____ ?

That would be you!

What Am I?

I come before **E**

But I am not **A**, **B**, or **C**

What letter am I?

Answer: _____

A B C D E

Buddy Letters

Fill in the letters
that rhyme. Use
the Letter Bank.

Letter Bank

A G I

B

K

Y

Name _____ Date _____

Letter Hunt

Write the missing letters. Use the Letter Bank.

Letter Bank

Cc	Hh	Ll	Oo	Rr	Vv
Ee	Jj	Mm	Qq	Tt	Zz

Aa	Bb		Dd		Ff
Gg		Ii		Kk	
	Nn		Pp		
Ss		Uu		Ww	Xx
		Yy			

Extra!

Circle the letter that begins your first name.

A   B   C   D   E

F   G   H   I   J   K

L   M   N   O   P

Q   R   S   T   U

V   W   X   Y   Z

Write the letter.

How Did You Do?

How many stars do you give your work? Color them.

Name _____ Date _____

Words to Know

Look at each pair of pictures. Say the names.
Listen to the rhymes.

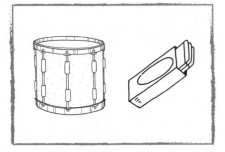

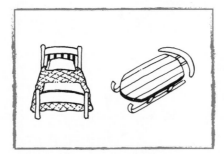

Extra!

Think of two new rhyming words.
Draw the pictures.

Name _____ Date _____

Kittens and Mittens

Help the kittens find their mittens. Help the other animals, too. Say the name for each animal. Color the picture that makes a rhyme.

Puzzle Play

Say the name for each picture.
Draw a line to match the rhyming pictures.

1.

2.

3.

4.

Buddy Words

Say the name for each picture.
Color the pictures that rhyme.

Thumbs Up!

Say the name for each picture. Do they rhyme? Color 👍 or 👎.

Name _____ Date _____

Fill-In Rhyme

Read the rhyme. Fill in the missing words. Use the Word Bank.

Word Bank

spoon   fiddle   moon

Hey, Diddle, Diddle

Hey, Diddle, Diddle,

The cat and the  _____

The cow jumped over the 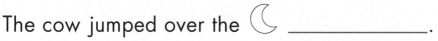 _____.

The little dog laughed to see such fun

And the dish ran away with the _____.

What Am I?

I rhyme with 🌙 .

My letters are the same both ways.

What word am I?

Answer: ____ ____ ____ ____

Use these letters:

o n o n

Name _____ Date _____

Bubble Time

Say the name for each picture.
Fill in the ○ for the rhyming picture.

1.   ○
   ○

2.    ○
   ○

3.    ○
   ○

4.    ○
   ○

How Did You Do?

How many stars do you give your work?
Color them.

Name _____ Date _____

Words to Know

Look at each pair of pictures. Say the names.
Listen to the rhymes.

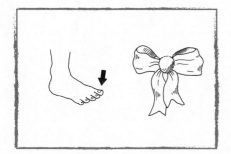 

Extra!

Think of two new rhyming words.
Draw the pictures.

My Checklist

✔ **Check each activity when you complete it.**

Page 1

_____ Words to Know

_____ Extra!

Page 2

_____ Rhyme Time

_____ What Doesn't Belong?

Page 3

_____ Puzzle Play

_____ Thumbs Up!

_____ Buddy Words

Page 4

_____ Fill-In Rhyme

_____ Extra!

Page 5

_____ Review

Name _____ Date _____

Rhyme Time

Say the name for the picture at the top of each box. Color the picture to make a rhyme.

What Doesn't Belong?

Say the name for each picture. **X** the picture that does not rhyme.

Name _____ Date _____

Rhyming Words (Packet 2)

Page **3**

Puzzle Play

Say the name for each picture.
Draw a line to match the rhyming picture.

1.

2.

3.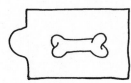

4.

Buddy Words

Say the name for each picture.
Color the rhyming buddies.

Thumbs Up!

Say the name for each picture. Do they rhyme? Color 👍 or 👎.

Name _____ Date _____

Fill-In Rhyme

Read the rhyme. Color the rhyming pictures to complete the poem.

One, Two, Buckle My Shoe

One **1**, two **2**,

buckle my

Three **3**, four **4**,

knock at the

Five **5**, six **6**,

pick up

Seven **7**, eight **8**,

lay them straight

Nine **9**, ten **10**,

a good fat   .

Say the name for each picture. Write the number that rhymes. Use the Number Bank.

Number Bank

1   8   3

 _____

 _____

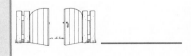 _____

Name _____ Date _____

Bubble Time

Say the name for each picture.

Fill in the ○ for the rhyming picture.

1. ○
   ○

2.  ○
   ○

3. ○
   ○

4.  ○
   ○

How Did You Do?

How many stars do you give your work?
Color them.

Extra!

Look at the pictures. Say the words. Color the pictures that rhyme.

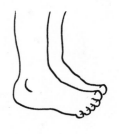

Name _____ Date _____

Words to Know

Say the words. Listen to the beginning sound.
Listen to the ending sound.

bed

cat

dog

run

six

web

Word Sort

Look at the words above. Write them in the boxes.

Words That Begin With *b, r, w*
_____
_____
_____

Words That End With *g, t, x*
_____
_____
_____

Name _____ Date _____

Lost and Found

What's in the Lost and Found? Say the name for each picture. Circle the letter that completes each word. Write it in the blank.

l k m

boo____

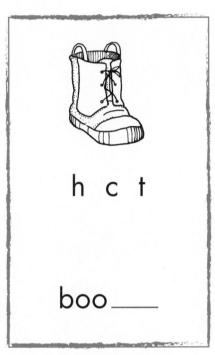

h c t

boo____

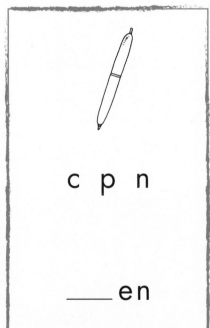

c p n

____en

s d n

____ock

Missing Letters

Look at the picture. Fill in the missing letters. Use the Letter Bank. Read the sentence.

Letter Bank

b p

I found my

ca____ and

my ____at!

Name _____ Date _____

Two-Way Words

Look at the pictures. Fill in the missing letter to make words both ways. Use the Letter Bank.

Make New Words

Look at each picture. Read the word. Change one letter to make a new word. Use the Letter Bank.

Letter Bank

f m s t

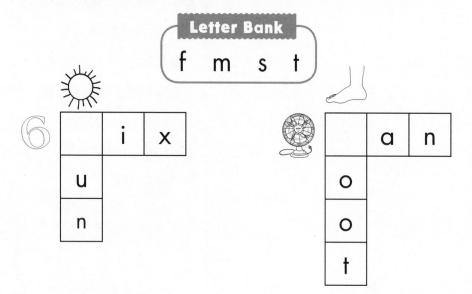

6

	i	x
u		
n		

	a	n
o		
o		
t		

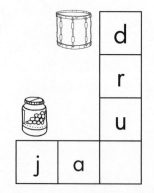

| d |
| r |
| u |
| j | a |

| g |
| o |
| a |
| t | e | n |

Letter Bank

f n

1. r u n

   __ u n

2. c a t

   c a __

Challenge Word

Fill in the missing letters.
Read the word.

__ p i __ e r

Use these letters:
d s

Week-by-Week Phonics Packets © 2010 by Joan Novelli and Holly Grundon. Scholastic Teaching Resources

Name _____ Date _____

Fill-In Story

Look at the pictures. Fill in the missing letters. Use the Letter Bank. Then read the story!

Letter Bank

p   d   g   f   c

A Noisy Farm

"Moo, moo," says the _____ow  .

"Baa, baa," says the shee_____  .

"Oink, oink," says the pi_____  .

"Quack, quack," says the _____uck  .

What a noisy _____arm!

What Am I?

When I am a baby
I am called a kid.
But I am not a person.
What am I?
Answer: a ____ o a ____

Use these letters:

t g

Buddy Words

Say the name for each picture. Fill in the missing letter. Use the Letter Bank.

Letter Bank

n   c   h

___at

___orse

he___

Week-by-Week Phonics Packets © 2010 by Joan Novelli and Holly Grundon. Scholastic Teaching Resources

29

Bubble Time

Say the name for each picture. Fill in the ○ to spell the word. Write the letter in the blank.

1.  ____og

   ○ d
   ○ z
   ○ h

2. ____ake

   ○ f
   ○ c
   ○ j

3. lea____

   ○ s
   ○ f
   ○ n

4. fla____

   ○ t
   ○ m
   ○ g

How Did You Do?

How many stars do you give your work?
Color them.

Thumbs Up!

Say the name for each picture. Does it begin with *s*? Color 👍 or 👎.

Name _____ Date _____

Words to Know

Some words have the short-*a* sound like *cat* .
Look at the pictures. Say the words. Listen to
the short-*a* sound. Underline the short *a* in
each word.

alligator

apple

cat

fan

jam

map

Word Sort

Look at the words above. Write them in the boxes.

Begins With Short **a**	Has Short **a** in the Middle
_____	_____
_____	_____
	_____

Name _____ Date _____

A Snack for Cat

Cat likes snacks with the short-*a* sound.
Look at the pictures in each box.
Say the words. Listen for the short-*a* sound.
Color the snacks that Cat likes.

32   *Week-by-Week Phonics Packets* © 2010 by Joan Novelli and Holly Grundon. Scholastic Teaching Resources

Missing Letters

Look at the picture. Fill in the missing letters. Use the Letter Bank. Read the sentence.

Letter Bank

a a t t

C _____ _____

is on the

h _____ _____!

Name _____ Date _____

Spelling Scramble

Say the name for each picture.
Unscramble the letters to spell the word.

1. a m p ___ ___ ___

2. c t a ___ ___ ___

3. j m a ___ ___ ___

4. n f a ___ ___ ___

5. e p p a l ___ ___ ___ ___ ___

Challenge Word

Fill in the missing letters.
Read the word.

Use these letters:
r a i

___ l l ___ g a t o ___

Shape Match

Look at each word. Find the matching shape. Fill in the letters. Read the words.

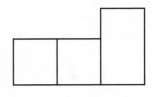
fan   map

cat   jam

Name _____ Date _____

Riddle Time

Read the riddles. Fill in the missing words.
Use the Word Bank.

Word Bank

ham   van   rat   cap

1. I rhyme with *cat.*

   I am a _____.

2. I rhyme with *jam.*

   I am a _____.

3. I rhyme with *map.*

   I am a _____.

4. I rhyme with *fan.*

   I am a _____.

What Am I?

I am not a cat.
I am not a rat.
I am a ____ ____ ____!

Extra!

Say the name for each picture. Color the pictures that rhyme.

Name _____ Date _____

Word Hunt

Write the word for each picture.
Use the Word Bank.

Word Bank

apple   cat   ham   map   rat   van

 _____

 _____

 _____

 _____

 _____

 _____

Find and circle the words.

a	c	a	t	m
p	c	h	a	a
p	v	a	n	p
l	m	h	a	m
e	r	a	t	p

How Did You Do?

How many stars do you give your work?
Color them.

What Doesn't Belong?

Look at the pictures in each row. Say the names. **X** the picture that does not have the short-*a* sound.

Words to Know

Some words have the short-e sound like *ten* 10. Look at the pictures. Say the words. Listen to the short-e sound. Underline the short e in each word.

bed   bell   hen

nest   net   tent

Word Sort

Look at the words above. Write them in the boxes.

Words With **3** Letters	Words With **4** Letters
_____	_____
_____	_____
_____	_____

Name _____ Date _____

Hen's Nest

Hen likes the short-e sound. Say the names for the pictures in each box. Listen for the short-e sound. Color the short-e pictures.

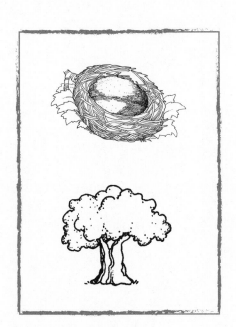

Week-by-Week Phonics Packets © 2010 by Joan Novelli and Holly Grundon. Scholastic Teaching Resources

37

Missing Letters

Look at the picture. Fill in the missing letters. Use the Letter Bank. Read the sentence.

Letter Bank

e   h

There is

a ___ en

on the

b ___ d!

Name _____ Date _____

Spelling Scramble

Say the name for each picture.
Unscramble the letters to spell the word.

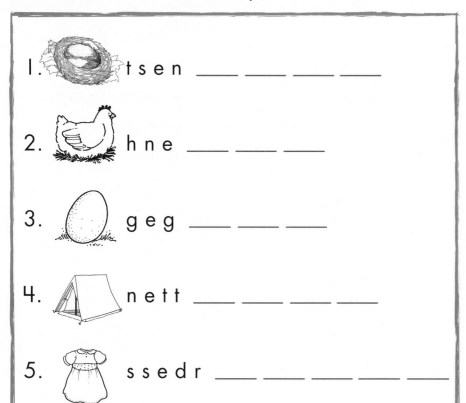

1. t s e n _____ _____ _____ _____

2. h n e _____ _____ _____

3. g e g _____ _____ _____

4. n e t t _____ _____ _____ _____

5. s s e d r _____ _____ _____ _____ _____

Challenge Word

Fill in the missing letters.
Read the word.

Use these letters:
e t e

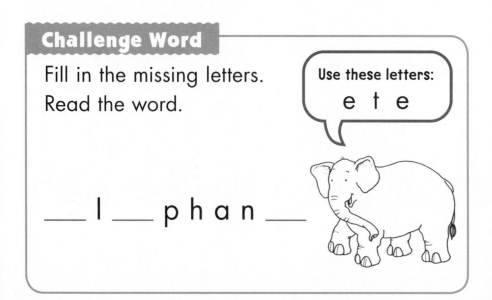

___ l ___ p h a n ___

Thumbs Up!

Say the name for each picture. Do you hear the short-e sound? Color or .

Name _____ Date _____

Riddle Time

Read the riddles. Use the words in the
Word Bank to fill in the blanks.

Word Bank

cent   tent   red   nest

1. I rhyme with bed.

   I am the color _____.

2. I am a home for an egg.

   I am a _____.

3. I am the same as a penny.

   I am one _____.

4. I begin and end the same.

   _____ is my name.

What Am I?

I can help you write.

I am also a home for a pig.

What am I?

Answer: a ____ ____ ____

Use these letters:

e p n

What Doesn't Belong?

Look at each
picture. Say the
words. ✗ the
word that does
not belong.

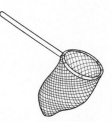

net   bell

win   web

Name _____ Date _____

Word Hunt

Write the word for each picture.
Use the Word Bank.

Word Bank

bed   dress   egg   nest   ten   web

 10 _____   _____

 _____   _____

 _____    _____

Find and circle
the words.

w	e	b	k	d
n	e	e	b	r
e	g	c	e	e
s	g	r	d	s
t	t	e	n	s

Bubble Time

Look at the picture. Fill in the ○ for the sentence that tells about the picture.

○ This room is a mess!

○ This room is a mop!

How Did You Do?

How many stars do you give your work?
Color them.  ☆ ☆ ☆ ☆ ☆

Name _____ Date _____

Words to Know

Some words have the short-*i* sound like *six* 6.
Say the name for each picture. Listen to the
short-*i* sound. Underline the short *i* in each word.

fish

milk

pig

pin

ship

zip

Word Sort

Look at the words above. Write them in the boxes.

Words With **3** Letters
_____
_____
_____

Words With **4** Letters
_____
_____
_____

My Checklist

✔ **Check each
activity when
you complete it.**

Page 1

_____ Words to Know

_____ Word Sort

Page 2

_____ Pig's Pictures

_____ Missing Letters

Page 3

_____ Spelling Scramble

_____ Make New Words

_____ Challenge Word

Page 4

_____ Fill-In Story

_____ Bubble Time

Page 5

_____ Review

Pig's Pictures

Pig paints pictures. He only paints pictures of the short-*i* sound. Say the name for each picture. Listen for the short-*i* sound. Circle the word, then write it.

fox   fish

_____

show   ship

_____

soap   sink

_____

milk   make

_____

Name _____ Date _____

Spelling Scramble

Say the name for each picture.
Unscramble the letters to spell the word.

1. f s h i ___ ___ ___ ___

2. i p g ___ ___ ___

3. i c k c h ___ ___ ___ ___ ___

4. x s i ___ ___ ___

5. k i m l ___ ___ ___ ___

Make New Words

Look at each picture. Read the word. Change the middle letter to *i*. Read your new words.

1.  d o g

   d ___ g

2. f a n

   f ___ n

3.  b a g

   b ___ g

4. p e n

   p ___ n

Challenge Word

Fill in the missing letters.
Read the word.

Use these letters:
i n e

p ___ n g u ___ ___

Name _____ Date _____

Fill-In Story

Look at the Word Bank. Use the words to fill in the blanks. Then read the story!

Word Bank

will   hill   skip   kick   swim

Bubble Time

Look at the picture. Fill in the ○ to tell one more way Pig and Chick have fun.

Pig and Chick Are Friends

"What will we do today, Chick?" asked Pig.

"We will climb the _____," said Chick.

"We will _____ the ball," said Pig.

"We will _____ rope," said Chick.

"We _____ be hot and tired!" said Pig.

"We will go for a _____!" said Chick.

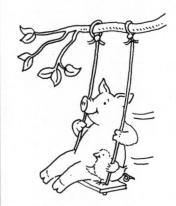

○ run

○ swing

○ walk

Name _____ Date _____

Word Hunt

Write the word for each picture.
Use the Word Bank.

Word Bank

| fish | milk | pin | ship | six | zip |

 _____   _____

 _____    _____

 _____   _____

Find and circle the words.

f	s	i	x	m
i	z	a	p	i
s	i	w	i	l
h	p	r	n	k
s	h	i	p	s

Say the name for each picture. **✗** the pictures that do not have the short-*i* sound.

How Did You Do?

How many stars do you give your work?
Color them.

Name _____ Date _____

Words to Know

Some words have the short-*o* sound like *sock* 🧦.
Say the name for each picture. Listen to the
short-*o* sound. Underline the short *o* in each word.

box   doll   fox

sock   stop   top

My Checklist

✔ **Check each activity when you complete it.**

Page 1
_____ Words to Know
_____ Word Sort

Page 2
_____ A Toy Box for Fox
_____ Missing Letters

Page 3
_____ Spelling Scramble
_____ Shape Match
_____ Challenge Word

Page 4
_____ Fill-In Rhyme
_____ What Am I?
_____ Extra!

Page 5
_____ Review

Word Sort

Look at the words above. Write them in the boxes.

Words With 3 Letters	Words With 4 Letters
_____	_____
_____	_____
_____	_____

A Toy Box for Fox

Fox's favorite toys have the short-o sound. Look at the pictures. Say the words. Listen for the short-o sound. Circle the word, then write it.

boat block

_____

frog flag

_____

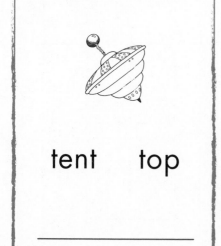

tent top

_____

doll duck

_____

Missing Letters

Look at the picture. Fill in the missing letters. Use the Letter Bank. Read the sentence.

Letter Bank

o x

Fo____

is in the

s____ck!

Name _____ Date _____

Spelling Scramble

Say the name for each picture.
Unscramble the letters to spell the word.

1.  f x o ___ ___ ___

2. o p s t ___ ___ ___ ___

3. o p s h ___ ___ ___ ___

4. o c k b l ___ ___ ___ ___ ___

5. o s k c ___ ___ ___ ___

Challenge Word

Fill in the missing letters.
Read the word.

Use these letters:
t   p   o

___ c ___ o ___ u s

Shape Match

Look at each word. Find the matching shape. Fill in the letters. Read the words.

 hot   not

pop   top

Fill-In Rhyme

Use the Word Bank to fill in the blanks.
Read your poem!

Word Bank

frog   hop   log   top

Fox and Frog

"Let's race," said the fox to the _____.

"We will race up and over that _____!

Can you jog all the way to the _____?"

"I can't jog," said the frog. "But I'll _____."

What Am I?

I am the opposite of *go*.
I don't mean *slow*.
What am I?
Answer: ____ ____ ____ ____

Use these letters:
t p o s

Name _____ Date _____

Word Hunt

Write the word for each picture.
Use the Word Bank.

Word Bank

box   doll   fox   sock   stop   top

 _____    _____

 _____   _____

 _____    _____

Find and circle
the words.

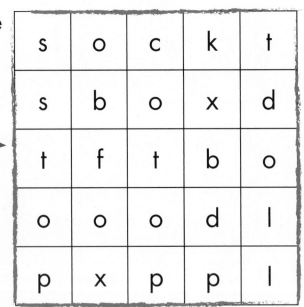

s	o	c	k	t
s	b	o	x	d
t	f	t	b	o
o	o	o	d	l
p	x	p	p	l

How Did You Do?

How many stars do you give your work?
Color them.

What Doesn't Belong?

Say the name
for each picture.
X the picture
that does not
have the short-o
sound.

Words to Know

Some words have the short-*u* sound like *sun* .
Look at the pictures. Say the words. Listen to the
short-*u* sound. Underline the *u* in each word.

bus

drum

duck

rug

skunk

truck

Word Sort

Look at the words above. Write them in the boxes.

Words With 3 Letters

_____   _____

Words With 4 Letters

_____   _____

Words With 5 Letters

_____   _____

My Checklist

✔ **Check each
activity when
you complete it.**

Page 1

_____ Words to Know

_____ Word Sort

Page 2

_____ Bug's Busy Day

_____ Missing Letters

Page 3

_____ Spelling Scramble

_____ Buddy Words

_____ Challenge Word

Page 4

_____ Fill-In Rhyme

_____ Make New Words

_____ What Am I?

Page 5

_____ Review

Bug's Busy Day

Bug had a busy day! Say the name for each picture. Circle the word, then write it. Use the words to tell a story about Bug's busy day.

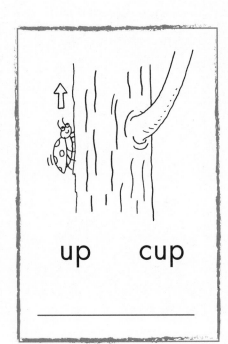

up   cup

_____

run   bun

_____

juggle   just

_____

tub   tug

_____

Missing Letters

Look at the picture. Fill in the missing letters. Use the Letter Bank. Read the sentence.

Letter Bank

g b u

As

sn ___ g

as a ___ ug

in a ru ___ !

Name _____ Date _____

Spelling Scramble

Say the name for each picture.
Unscramble the letters to spell the word.

1. s b u ___ ___ ___

2. c k t r u ___ ___ ___ ___ ___

3. m u d r ___ ___ ___ ___

4. u m g ___ ___ ___

5. k c d u ___ ___ ___ ___

Buddy Words

Fill in the missing letters. Use the Letter Bank. Read your words.

Letter Bank

g   s   r

 ___un

 bu___

 ___un

Challenge Word

Fill in the missing letters. Read the word.

Use these letters:
t   f   u

b ___ t ___ e r ___ l y

Name _____ Date _____

Fill-In Rhyme

Fill in the letter *u* to complete each word.
Read the rhyme.

Where Is Short *u*?

What words have short *u*?

D____ck and tr____ck 🚚 are two.

There's a short *u* in s____n ☀ .

It's in r____n 🏃 and in f____n.

But with dr____m 🥁

you hear rat-a-tat **BOOM!**

What Am I?

I am a baby bear,

And a baby fox, too.

What letters spell my name?

They are b, c, and u.

Answer: a ____ ____ ____

Make New Words

Look at each picture. Read the word. Change the *a* to *u* and write it in the blank. Read your new words.

1. 🦇 b a t

   b <u>u</u> t

2. 🌀 f a n

   f __ n

3. 🛍 b a g

   b __ g

4. 🧢 c a p

   c __ p

Name _____ Date _____

Word Hunt

Write the word for each picture.
Use the Word Bank.

Word Bank

| bug | bus | drum | rug | skunk | sun |

 _____

 _____

 _____

 _____

 _____

_____

Find and circle the words.

b	u	g	d	r
b	s	b	r	u
u	u	e	u	g
s	n	c	m	v
s	k	u	n	k

How Did You Do?

How many stars do you give your work?
Color them.

☆ ☆ ☆ ☆ ☆

What Doesn't Belong?

Say the name for each picture.
✗ the pictures that do not have the short-*u* sound.

Words to Know

A vowel can sound like its name. This is called a long-vowel sound. Look at the pictures. Say the words. Listen for letters that sound like their name. Underline *a* and *i*.

bike

cake

gate

kite

mice

rake

Word Sort

Look at the words above. Write them in the boxes.

Words With **Long a**	Words With **Long i**
_____	_____
_____	_____
_____	_____

My Checklist

✔ **Check each activity when you complete it.**

Page 1

_____ Words to Know

_____ Word Sort

Page 2

_____ Whale's Birthday

_____ Missing Letters

Page 3

_____ What's the Word?

_____ Buddy Words

_____ Challenge Word

Page 4

_____ Riddle Time

_____ What Doesn't Belong?

Page 5

_____ Review

Name _____ Date _____

Whale's Birthday

It's Whale's birthday! Say the name for each picture. Circle the word, then write it. Use your words to tell a story about Whale's birthday.

cake   cone

_____

name   game

_____

bike   kite

_____

hide   slide

_____

Look at the picture. Fill in the missing letters. Use the Letter Bank. Read the sentence.

Letter Bank

i   a

Watch Wh ___ le

r ___ de the bike!

Name _____ Date _____

What's the Word?

Read each clue. Write the answer.
Use the Word Bank.

Word Bank

dine   face   five   game   lake

1. Has the little word *ace*: _____

2. The word for 5: _____

3. A way to say *eat*: _____

4. Bigger than a pond: _____

5. Something to play: _____

Buddy Words

Fill in the letters to spell each pair of words. Use the Letter Bank. Use each letter two times.

Letter Bank

a i

f__ve   n__ne

s__me   m__de

Challenge Word

Fill in the missing letters.
Read the word.

Use these letters:
e i o

c r o c __ d __ l __

Riddle Time

Read the riddles. Use the words in the Word Bank to fill in the blanks.

Word Bank

dice   grape   kite   nine

1. I can fly,

   But I don't have wings.

   I am a _____.

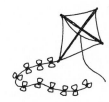

2. You can roll me,

   But I am not a ball.

   I am _____.

3. I come in a bunch,

   But I am not a banana.

   I am a _____.

4. I am less than 10,

   But more than 8.

   I am the number _____.

What Doesn't Belong?

Look at each picture. Say the words. **✗** the word that does not belong.

tape   ten

make   mice

Name _____ Date _____

Word Hunt

Write the word for each picture.
Use the Word Bank.

Word Bank

bike   five   mice   rake   skate   whale

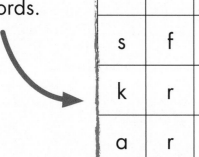 _____    _____

_____   _____

 _____    _____

Find and circle
the words.

m	i	c	e	r	w
s	f	i	v	e	h
k	r	t	s	o	a
a	r	a	k	e	l
t	w	d	f	c	e
e	b	b	i	k	e

How Did You Do?

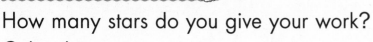

How many stars do you give your work?
Color them.

Extra!

Say the word
for each picture.
Write **A** for the
long-*a* sound.
Write **I** for the
long-*i* sound.

 _____

 _____

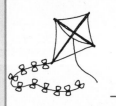 _____

 _____

Name _____ Date _____

Words to Know

A vowel can sound like its name. This is called a long-vowel sound. Look at the pictures. Say the words. Listen for the sound of *o* and *u*. Underline *o* and *u*.

bone

cone

cube

nose

mule

rose

Word Sort

Look at the words above. Write them in the boxes.

Words With **Long o**	Words With **Long u**
_____	_____
_____	_____
_____	_____
_____	

Week-by-Week Phonics Packets © 2010 by Joan Novelli and Holly Grundon. Scholastic Teaching Resources

My Checklist

✔ **Check each activity when you complete it.**

Page I

_____ Words to Know

_____ Word Sort

Page 2

_____ Doggie Wants a Bone

_____ Missing Letters

Page 3

_____ Two-Way Words

_____ What's the Word?

_____ Challenge Word

Page 4

_____ Fill-In Rhyme

_____ What Doesn't Belong?

_____ What Am I?

Page 5

_____ Review

Name _____ Date _____

Doggie Wants a Bone

Help Doggie find the bones.
Say the name for each picture.
Color the matching bone.
Read your words.

Look at the pictures. Fill in the missing letters. Use the Letter Bank. Read the sentence.

Letter Bank
e u e o

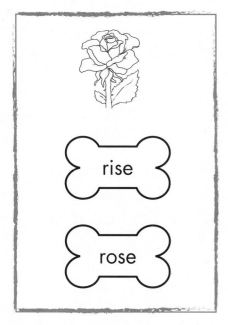

rise

rose

mice

mule

A c___n___ and a c___b___ are both shapes.

cone

cane

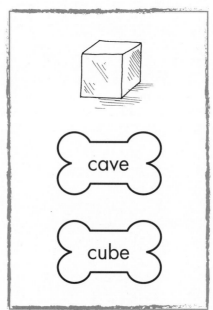

cave

cube

Two-Way Words

Look at the pictures. Fill in the missing letters to make words both ways. Use the Letter Bank. Write your words.

Letter Bank

u   o

```
    r
n   s   e
    s
    e
```

```
    c
c   t   e
    b
    e
```

_____

_____

_____

_____

Challenge Word

Fill in the missing letters.
Read the word.

Use these letters:

o   e

t e l __ p h __ n e

What's the Word?

Use the Word Bank to find the answers.

Word Bank

those

use

1. Add an *e* to *us* to make this word:

   _____

2. Has the little word *hose*:

   _____

Name _____ Date _____

Fill-In Rhyme

Look at the Word Bank. Use the words to fill in the blanks. Then read the story!

Word Bank

bone   flute   tune

What Can a Dog Do?

Can a dog hum a _____?

No, can you?

Can a dog dig for a _____?

Yes, that's true.

Can a dog play the _____

and the tuba, too?

No, a dog cannot.

But a dog can chew!

What Am I?

I belong on a face
But I am not your eyes.
I help you smell things
Like cakes and pies!
What am I?

Answer: a ____ ____ ____ ____

Use these letters:

o s n e

What Doesn't Belong?

Say the name for each picture. **X** the picture that does not have a long-*o* sound.

Name _____ Date _____

Word Hunt

Write the word for each picture.
Use the Word Bank.

Word Bank

bone   cone   cube   mule   nose   rose

 _____

 _____

 _____

 _____

 _____

 _____

Find and circle the words.

r	c	o	n	e	e
o	m	u	l	e	c
s	u	m	n	o	u
e	l	o	n	s	b
v	n	o	s	e	e
o	b	o	n	e	b

How Did You Do?

How many stars do you give your work?
Color them.

☆ ☆ ☆ ☆ ☆

Extra!

What's a word that tells about the puppy? Fill in the missing letters. Read the word.

Letter Bank

e   u

c __ t __

Name _____ Date _____

Words to Know

Some words have vowel teams. Vowel teams are two letters that have one sound. Look at the pictures. Say the words. Listen for the long-*a* sound. Underline *ai* and *ay*.

play   rain   spray

tail   train   tray

Word Sort

Look at the words above. Write them in the boxes.

Words With *ai*	Words With *ay*
_____	_____
_____	_____
_____	_____

Name _____ Date _____

Play Time

It's time to play! Say the name for each picture.
Circle the word, then write it. Use the words
to tell a story.

Look at the
picture. Fill in the
missing letters.
Use the Letter
Bank. Read the
sentence.

Letter Bank
a i a y

cake   clay

_____

rain   train

_____

It's fun to

pl__ __ in

the r__ __n!

paint   pet

_____

say   play

_____

Spelling Scramble

Say the name for each picture.
Unscramble the letters to spell the word.

1. a h y   ___ ___ ___

2. a l a i p   ___ ___ ___ ___

3. r b n a i   ___ ___ ___ ___ ___

4. a y t r   ___ ___ ___ ___

5. s l a i   ___ ___ ___ ___

Shape Match

Look at each word. Find the matching shape. Fill in the letters. Read the words.

day   way

tail

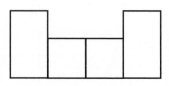

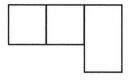

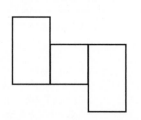

Challenge Word

Fill in the missing letters.
Read the word.

Use these letters:
s   y   a

c r ___ ___ o n ___

Name _____ Date _____

Fill-In Story

Look at the Word Bank. Use the words to fill in the blanks. Then read the story!

Word Bank

| mail | paint | say | today | wait |

It's My Birthday!

It's my birthday _____!

Look what came in the _____!

I can't _____ to open it!

Look at my new _____ set!

I will _____, "Thank you!"

Extra!

Look at the Word Bank. Find three words that have **ai**. Write them.

1. _____

2. _____

3. _____

What Am I?

To play this game you spin and spin.

Pin me in place and you might win.

What am I?

Answer: a ____ ____ ____ ____

Use these letters: a i l t

Name _____ Date _____

Word Hunt

Write the word for each picture. Use the Word Bank.

Word Bank

hay   play   rain   tail   train   tray

 _____

 _____

 _____

 _____

 _____

 _____

Find and circle the words.

t	r	a	i	n
h	t	a	i	l
a	r	a	i	n
y	p	l	a	y
t	r	a	y	y

How Did You Do?

How many stars do you give your work? Color them.

☆ ☆ ☆ ☆ ☆

Bubble Time

Say the name for each picture. Fill in the ○ to spell each word. Write the letters in the blanks.

1. sn___ ___l
   ○ ai
   ○ ay

2. h___ ___
   ○ ai
   ○ ay

Name _____ Date _____

Words to Know

Some words have vowel teams. Vowel teams are two letters that have one sound. Look at the pictures. Say the words. Listen for the long-*e* sound. Underline *ea* and *ee*.

bean

bee

cheese

dream

feet

leaf

Word Sort

Look at the words above. Write them in the boxes.

Words With *ea*	Words With *ee*
_____	_____
_____	_____
_____	_____

In the Garden

What's growing in this garden? Say the name for each picture. Circle the word, then write it. Use the words to tell a garden story.

seeds   sent

_____

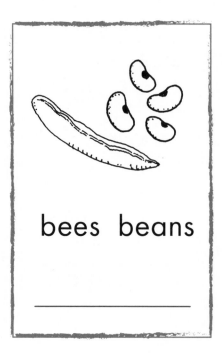

bees   beans

_____

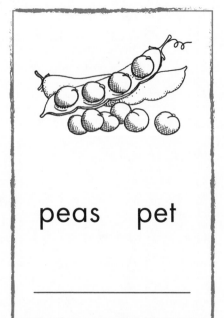

peas   pet

_____

books   beets

_____

Missing Letters

Look at the picture. Fill in the missing letters. Use the Letter Bank. Read the sentence.

Letter Bank

g e a

I wish ice cr___ ___m grew in ___ardens!

Vowel Teams (ea, ee)

Make New Words

Put letters together from each box to make words. Use the letters more than once. Write your words.

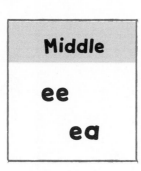

Beginning	
b	f
m	s

Middle
ee
ea

End	
t	l
n	m

1. _____b e a t_____   4. _____

2. _____   5. _____

3. _____   6. _____

Two-Way Words

Fill in the letter that spells a word each way. Use the Letter Bank.

Letter Bank

p   t

n	e	a	
		r	
		e	
		e	

	k	
	e	
	e	
l	e	a

Challenge Word

Fill in the missing letters. Read the word.

Use these letters:

e s e

t r ___ ___ h o u ___ e

Name _____ Date _____

Fill-In Story

Look at the Word Bank. Use the words to fill in the blanks. Then read the story!

Word Bank

sleep   sweet   three   bees

Sweet Dreams

"Little Bear, it's time for bed," said Mama Bear.

"_____ dreams."

"One, two, _____. Counting will

help me _____," said Little Bear.

"Are you counting sheep?" asked Mama Bear.

"No," said Little Bear.

"I am counting _____!"

Extra!

Look at the Word Bank. Write the word that tells how many.

_____

Name _____ Date _____

Word Hunt

Write the word for each picture.
Use the Word Bank.

Word Bank

bean   bee   feet   leaf   read   tree

 _____

 _____

 _____

Find and circle
the words.

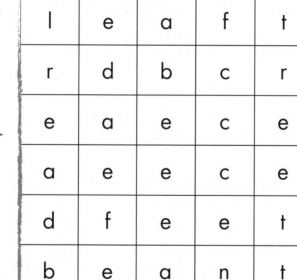

l	e	a	f	t
r	d	b	c	r
e	a	e	c	e
a	e	e	c	e
d	f	e	e	t
b	e	a	n	t

How Did You Do?

How many stars do you give your work?
Color them.

   ☆ ☆

Bubble Time

Say the word for
the picture. Fill
in the ○ for the
word.

○ drip

○ dream

○ bean

Name _____ Date _____

Words to Know

Some words have vowel teams. Vowel teams are two letters that have one sound. Look at the pictures. Say the words. Listen for the *oa*, *oe*, and *ow* sounds. Underline *oa*, *oe*, and *ow*.

boat

bow

goat

hoe

snow

toe

Word Sort

Look at the words above. Write them in the boxes.

Words With oa

_____   _____

Words With oe

_____   _____

Words With ow

_____   _____

Name _____ Date _____

Four Seasons on a Farm

What happens all year on the farm? Look at each picture. Circle the word, then write it. Use the words to tell a story about the farm.

Spring

hoe   hop

_____

Summer

boat   grow

_____

Fall

mow   more

_____

Winter

saw   snow

_____

Missing Letters

Look at the picture. Fill in the missing letters. Use the Letter Bank. Read the sentence.

Letter Bank

a   o

A baby horse is a f___ ___l.

Name _____ Date _____

What's the Word?

Read each clue. Write the answer.
Use the Word Bank.

Word Bank

foal   blow   oat   slow   toe

1. Not fast: _____

2. Something to eat: _____meal

3. The name for a young horse: _____

4. Has the little word *low*: _____

5. Sounds the same as *tow*: _____

Challenge Word

Fill in the missing letters.
Read the word.

Use these letters:
o   w   a

s h ___ d ___ ___

Make New Words

Look at each picture. Read the word. Change one letter to make a new word. Use the Letter Bank.

Letter Bank

l   g   k

b o a t

___ o a t

m o w

___ o w

s n o w

___ n o w

Riddle Time

Read the riddles. Look at the pictures. Fill in the missing words. Use the Word Bank.

Word Bank

boat   coat   snow   toe

1. I am made of water

   But you can't pour me.

   I am _____.

2. When you are cold,

   I am warm.

   I am a _____.

3. I am part of a foot

   But I'm not an inch.

   I am a _____.

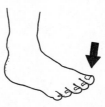

4. A ship is bigger than me

   But we both go on the sea.

   I am a _____.

What Doesn't Belong?

Look at each picture. Say the words. ✗ the word that does not belong.

crow   cow

sip   soap

Name _____ Date _____

Word Hunt

Write the word for each picture.
Use the Word Bank.

Word Bank

| bow | coat | hoe | goat | snow | toe |

  _____

  _____

_____

  _____

_____

_____

Find and circle the words.

s	n	o	w	g
c	b	o	w	o
o	t	g	d	a
a	o	r	a	t
t	e	h	o	e

How Did You Do?

How many stars do you give your work?
Color them. ☆ ☆ ☆ ☆ ☆

Bubble Time

Read the sentence. Fill in the ○ for the missing letters. Write the letters in the blanks.

A lamb gr___ ___s up to be a sheep.

○ oa

○ ow

○ oe

Name _____ Date _____

Words to Know

The letters *oo* can sound like *book* .
The letters *oo* can sound like *moon* .
Read the words. Listen for the *oo* sound.
Underline *oo*.

book   good   look   moon

room   soon   took   tooth

Word Sort

Look at the words above. Write them in the boxes.

OO Like *Book*	OO Like *Moon*
_____	_____
_____	_____
_____	_____
_____	_____

What's That Sound?

Look at each picture. Circle the word for the sound. Write the word in the speech bubble.

woof   wood

took   toot

soon   zoom

hoot   hop

Look at the picture. Fill in the missing letters. Use the Letter Bank. Read the sentence.

Letter Bank

o   g   o

"Would you like a c___ ___kie, Moose?" said ___oose.

Name _____ Date _____

Name _____ Date _____

What's the Word?

Read each clue. Write the answer.
Use the Word Bank.

Word Bank

boots   noon   took   tooth   wood

1. Has the same sound as *would*: _____

2. Has two letters that are short for *okay*: _____

3. More than one of these is *teeth*: _____

4. A pair has a left and a right: _____

5. Morning, ___?___, and night: _____

Buddy Words

Fill in the missing word parts. Use the Letter Bank. Read your words.

Letter Bank

good ool z

sch_____

_____oom

_____bye

Challenge Word

Fill in the missing letters.
Read the word.

Use these letters:

o k a o

___ a n g ___ r ___ ___

Name _____ Date _____

Riddle Time

Read the riddles. Write the answers.
Use the Word Bank.

Word Bank

balloon   book   food   wood

1. I come from a tree

   You can build with me.

   What am I?

   Answer: _____

2. Blow and blow, then you must stop

   If you don't, I might go **POP**!

   What am I?

   Answer: a _____

3. I am what you eat and drink.

   I can help you grow and think.

   What am I?

   Answer: _____

4. I have letters and pages.

   I am fun for all ages.

   What am I?

   Answer: a _____

Thumbs Up!

Say the name for each picture. Color 👍 if you hear **oo**. Color 👎 if you don't.

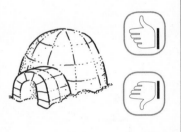

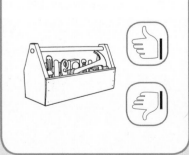

Name _____ Date _____

Word Tree

Think of words with the letters *oo*. Write them.

Words With **OO**

How many stars do you give your work?
Color them.

Bubble Time

Look at each picture. Fill in the ○ for the correct word.

1.

○ zip

○ zoo

○ so

2.

○ bring

○ brown

○ broom

Name _____ Date _____

Words to Know

Sometimes the letters *ou* make the sound in *cloud* ☁️. Sometimes the letters *ow* make the sound in *flower* 🌼. Read the words. Listen for the *ou* and *ow* sounds. Underline *ou* and *ow*.

cl<u>ou</u>d	count	down	flower
hour	how	now	out

Word Sort

Look at the words above. Write them in the boxes.

Words With OU ☁️

_____

_____

_____

_____

Words With OW 🌼

_____

_____

_____

_____

Name _____ Date _____

Bear Takes a Hike

What will Bear see on his hike?
Say the name for each picture.
Circle the word, then write it. Tell a
story about Bear's hike.

clouds   crowns

_____

flags   flowers

_____

moon   mouse

_____

owl   wall

_____

Missing Letters

Look at the picture. Fill in the missing letters. Use the Letter Bank. Read the sentence.

Letter Bank

g o r w

A wolf can bark,

__ __owl, and

h__ __l!

Name _____ Date _____

What's the Word?

Read each clue. Write the answer.
Use the Word Bank.

Word Bank

brown   now   hour   loud   south

1. Sounds like *our*: _____

2. A color word: _____

3. Another word for *noisy*: _____

4. Not later: _____

5. North, ___**?**___, east, and west: _____

Challenge Word

Fill in the missing letters.
Read the word.

Use these letters:
o   n   w

s u ___ f l ___ ___ e r

Buddy Words

Fill in the missing word parts. Use the Letter Bank. Read your words.

Letter Bank

f   bout   own

a _____

_____ ound

d _____

Fill-In Rhyme

Look at the Letter Bank. Use the letters to fill in the blanks. Then read the rhyme!

Letter Bank

ch   p   sc

A Grouchy Day

Are there times you growl?

Are there times you ___ ___owl?

Are there times you shout?

Are there times you ___out?

Are there times you're a grouch?

Are there times you say ou___ ___?

What do you do then?

Try counting to **10**!

Extra!

Look at the picture. Fill in **ou** or **ow** to spell the word.

c__ __ch

89

Name _____ Date _____

Word Tree

Think of words with the letters *ou* and *ow*.
Write them.

Words With
OU and **OW**

 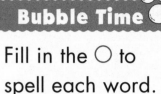
Fill in the ○ to spell each word. Write the letters in the blanks.

1. ab____ ____t
   - ○ ou
   - ○ ow

2. ar____ ____nd
   - ○ ow
   - ○ ou

3. d____ ____n
   - ○ ou
   - ○ ow

How Did You Do?

How many stars do you give your work?
Color them.

Name _____ Date _____

Words to Know

Some words have a vowel with the letter *r*.
Car has *ar*. These letters make a sound together. Read the words. Underline the vowel + *r*.

bird

car

fork

girl

horse

star

Word Sort

Look at the words above. Write them in the boxes.

Words With *ar*

_____   _____

Words With *ir*

_____   _____

Words With *or*

_____   _____

Week-by-Week Phonics Packets © 2010 by Joan Novelli and Holly Grundon. Scholastic Teaching Resources

My Checklist

✔ **Check each activity when you complete it.**

Page 1

_____ Words to Know

_____ Word Sort

Page 2

_____ Let's Go to a Farm

_____ Missing Letters

Page 3

_____ What's the Word?

_____ Make New Words

_____ Challenge Word

Page 4

_____ Fill-In Story

_____ Extra!

Page 5

_____ Review

Name _____ Date _____

Let's Go to a Farm

What can you find on a farm? Say the name for each picture. Circle the word, then write it. Tell a story about a farm.

flower   farmer

_____

bear   horse

_____

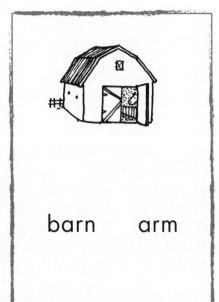

barn   arm

_____

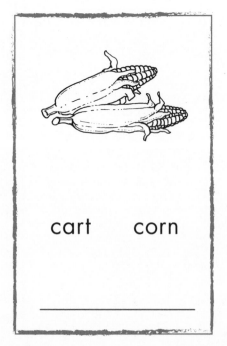

cart   corn

_____

Name _____ Date _____

What's the Word?

Read each clue. Write the answer.
Use the Word Bank.

Word Bank

chart   dirt   far   first   for

1. Sounds like *four*: _____

2. Not *near*: _____

3. The word for 1st: _____

4. A word for *soil*: _____

5. Has the little word *art*: _____

Make New Words

Choose letters from the Letter Bank to make words. You can use letters more than once. Write your words.

Letter Bank

b c e k n
s sh st t

1. _b_ ar _k_

_____ ar _t_

_____ ar _____

2. _s_ or _t_

_____ or _n_

_____ or _____

Challenge Word

Fill in the missing letters.
Read the word.

Use these letters:
f   i   r

g ___ ___ a f ___ e

Fill-In Story

Read the story. Choose the missing letters.
Fill in the blank to spell the words.

All About Acorns

Acorns grow on oak trees.

An **ac_____n** is a seed in a shell.
  or   ir

Acorns _____**e** food for some animals.
  ir   ar

Bluejays and other **b_____ds** eat acorns.
  ar   ir

Squ_____rels eat acorns, too.
  ir   ar

They **st_____e** acorns in the ground.
  or   ir

The acorns are food **f_____** winter.
  ar   or

But not all acorns are eaten.

Some grow into trees!

Extra!

Look at the story. Find two words that rhyme with **more**. Write them.

1. _____

2. _____

Name _____ Date _____

Word Tree

Think of words with the letters *ar*, *ir*, and *or*.
Write them.

Words With
ar,
ir, and **or**

Bubble Time

Say the name for each picture. Fill in the ○ for the word.

1.
   ○ store
   ○ shore

2.
   ○ yarn
   ○ yard

2.
   ○ shark
   ○ shirt

Name _____ Date _____

Words to Know

Some words have letters that go together.
The letters *c* and *l* go together in *cloud* .
Read the words. Listen for the sounds of *bl*, *cl*,
fl, *gl*, *pl*, and *sl*. Underline the letters.

block

clock

flag

glue

plate

sled

Word Sort

Look at the words above. Write them in the boxes.

Words With *bl, fl, pl*	Words With *cl, gl, sl*
_____	_____
_____	_____
_____	_____

Name _____ Date _____

Flashlight Fun

What do you see in each box?
Circle the word, then write it.

clock   cloth

_____

ships   slippers

_____

blue   blanket

_____

glass   grapes

_____

Missing Letters

Look at the picture. Fill in the missing letters. Use the Letter Bank. Read the sentence.

Letter Bank

sl   sh

You can count

_____eep

when you go

to _____eep.

Name _____ Date _____

What's the Word?

Read each clue. Write the answer.
Use the Word Bank.

Word Bank

clue   flour   glad   place   sleeve

1. Has the same sound as *flower*: _____

2. Part of a shirt: _____

3. A hint or sign: _____

4. A word for *happy*: _____

5. Has the little word *lace*: _____

Challenge Word

Fill in the missing letters.
Read the word.

Use these letters:

g l r

p ___ a y ___ ___ o u n d

Buddy Words

Fill in the missing letters. Use the Letter Bank. Read your words.

Letter Bank

cl   ip   sl

fl _____

_____ ow

_____ ean

Name _____ Date _____

Riddle Time

Read the riddles. Look at the pictures. Fill in the blanks. Use the Word Bank.

Word Bank

cloud   flashlight   globe   sled

1. You can see me float around.

   I am found above the ground.

   I am a _____.

2. I am a kind of map.

   I am round, not flat.

   I am a _____.

3. When I go for a ride

   I slip and I slide.

   I am a _____.

4. When it's dark I give light.

   You can use me at night.

   I am a _____.

Extra!

Look at the pictures. Fill in the missing letters to spell the words. Use the Letter Bank.

Letter Bank

bl   pl

_____ug

_____ow

Name _____ Date _____

Word Hunt

Write the word for each picture.
Use the Word Bank.

Word Bank

block   cloud   flag   glue   plug   sled

 _____

 _____

 _____

 _____

Find and circle the words.

b	f	l	a	g	a
l	s	e	g	r	c
o	l	b	l	s	l
c	e	a	u	v	o
k	d	s	e	r	u
r	p	l	u	g	d

How Did You Do?

How many stars do you give your work?
Color them.

100   *Week-by-Week Phonics Packets* © 2010 by Joan Novelli and Holly Grundon. Scholastic Teaching Resources

Bubble Time

Fill in the ○ to spell each word. Write the letters in the blanks.

1. _____ack

   ○ gl
   ○ bl

2. _____ease

   ○ pl
   ○ cl

3. _____eep

   ○ sl
   ○ fl

Name _____ Date _____

Words to Know

Some words have letters that go together. The letters c and r go together in crown . Read the words. Listen for the sounds of br, cr, dr, gr, pr, and tr. Underline the letters.

bread

crown

dragon

grass

pretzel

triangle

Word Sort

Look at the words above. Write them in the boxes.

Words With br, pr, dr	Words With cr, gr, tr
_____	_____
_____	_____
_____	_____

Name _____ Date _____

Dragon's Favorite Things

What are Dragon's favorite things?
Look at the picture in each box.
Circle the word, then write it. Tell a
story about Dragon's favorite things!

Missing Letters

Look at the
picture. Fill in the
missing letters.
Use the Letter
Bank. Read the
sentence.

Letter Bank

tr   dr

_____agon

likes to take

the _____ain.

Favorite Shape

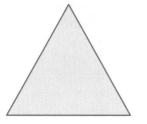

triangle square

_____

Favorite Animal

from   frog

_____

Favorite Food

brook   bread

_____

Favorite Friend

princess   print

_____

Name _____ Date _____

What's the Word?

Read each clue. Write the answer.
Use the Word Bank.

Word Bank

crowd   Friday   grin   price   train

1. How much something costs: _____

2. Has the little word *rain*: _____

3. A word for *smile*: _____

4. A day of the week: _____

5. Lots of people in one place: _____

Challenge Word

Fill in the missing letters.
Read the word.

Use these letters:
s   f   r

___ ___ i e n d ___

Buddy Words

Fill in the missing letters. Use the Letter Bank. Read your words.

Letter Bank

aw   br   om

fr _____

_____ ing

dr _____

Name _____ Date _____

Fill-In Rhyme

Fill in the missing letters. Use the Letter Bank.
Read the rhyme!

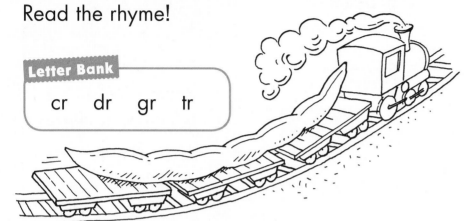

Letter Bank

cr   dr   gr   tr

The Great Green Bean

There was a _____**een** bean

as big as a _____**agon**.

It would not fit on a cart or a wagon.

The farmer then tried

a truck, then a _____**ane**.

And at last put the bean

on a very big _____**ain**.

Look at the Fill-In Rhyme. Write the words you made.

1. _____

2. _____

3. _____

4. _____

Bubble Time

Look at each picture. Fill in the ○ to spell the word. Write the letters in the blanks.

1. _____ize
   - ○ pr
   - ○ bl

2. _____y
   - ○ gr
   - ○ cr

3. _____uit
   - ○ tr
   - ○ fr

4. _____unk
   - ○ tr
   - ○ gr

How Did You Do?

How many stars do you give your work? Color them.

What Doesn't Belong?

Look at the pictures in each box. **X** the one that doesn't belong.

br

cr

tr

Words to Know

Some words have letters that go together. The letters *s* and *m* go together in *smile* . Read the words. Listen for the sounds of *sc*, *sk*, *sm*, *sn*, *sp*, and *st*. Underline the letters.

scarf

skate

smile

snake

spoon

stove

Word Sort

Look at the words above. Write them in the boxes.

Words With sc, sp, sm	Words With sk, sn, st
_____	_____
_____	_____
_____	_____

My Checklist

✔ Check each activity when you complete it.

Page 1

_____ Words to Know

_____ Word Sort

Page 2

_____ Skunk's Snazzy Sneakers

_____ Missing Letters

Page 3

_____ What's the Word?

_____ Buddy Words

_____ Challenge Word

Page 4

_____ Fill-In-Story

_____ Extra!

Page 5

_____ Review

Name _____ Date _____

Skunk's Snazzy Sneakers

Skunk likes sneakers! Look at each pair of sneakers. Circle the word, then write it. Color the sneakers!

stripes

states

_____

spins

spots

_____

stars

stops

_____

snowman

snowflakes

_____

Missing Letters

Look at the picture. Fill in the missing letters. Use the Letter Bank. Read the sentence.

Letter Bank

sc   sk

_____unk

likes to ride on

her _____ooter.

Name _____ Date _____

What's the Word?

Read each clue. Write the answer.
Use the Word Bank.

Word Bank

skill   smell   snack   speak   stack

1. To talk: _____

2. One of the five senses: _____

3. A pile of things: _____

4. A small meal: _____

5. Something you learn: _____

Challenge Word

Fill in the missing letters.
Read the word.

Use these letters:
b   r   t

s ___ ___ a w ___ e r r y

Buddy Words

Fill in the missing letters. Use the Letter Bank. Read your words.

Letter Bank

sm   ore   sw

sc _____

_____ ile

_____ eet

Fill-In Story

Fill in the missing words. Use the
Word Bank. Then read the story!

Word Bank

skunk   Snake

Squirrel

spots   stripe

Look at the
Word Bank. Find
the words. Then
write them.

1. A word with
   double *r*:

   _____

2. A word that
   begins and
   ends with *s*:

   _____

3. A word that
   rhymes with
   take:

   _____

Little Skunk's Stripe

"Snake, have you seen my stripe?"

asked Little Skunk.

"No," said _____, and he slid away.

"Squirrel, have you seen my

_____?" asked Little Skunk.

"No," said _____, and he hopped away.

Then Mother Skunk came along.

"Have you seen my stripe?" asked Little Skunk.

"Little Skunk, you didn't lose your stripe!

You have black and white _____.

You are a spotted _____!"

Name _____ Date _____

Bubble Time

Look at each picture. Fill in the ○ for the beginning sound.

1.
   ○ sk
   ○ sl
   ○ sp

2.
   ○ sm
   ○ sl
   ○ sp

3.
   ○ sk
   ○ sn
   ○ sp

4.
   ○ st
   ○ sn
   ○ sp

5.
   ○ sw
   ○ st
   ○ sn

6.
   ○ sc
   ○ st
   ○ sn

How Did You Do?

How many stars do you give your work?
Color them.

What Doesn't Belong?

Look at the pictures in each box. **X** the one that does not belong.

st

sc

sp

Name _____ Date _____

Words to Know

Sometimes two letters make one sound together. The letters *s* and *h* go together in fish . Say the name for each picture. Listen for the sounds of *sh* and *wh*. Underline *sh* and *wh*.

fish

shadow

wash

whale

wheel

whistle

Word Sort

Look at the words above. Write them in the boxes.

Words With *sh*	Words With *wh*
_____	_____
_____	_____
_____	_____

My Checklist

✔ **Check each activity when you complete it.**

Page 1

_____ Words to Know

_____ Word Sort

Page 2

_____ What Do You See at Sea?

_____ Missing Letters

Page 3

_____ What's the Word?

_____ Make New Words

_____ Challenge Word

Page 4

_____ Fill–In Story

_____ Extra!

Page 5

_____ Review

What Do You See at Sea?

Let's go to the sea! What will you see? Say the name for the picture in each box. Choose the missing letters. Write them in the blank.

____ip

(sh) (wh)

____ark

(sh) (wh)

____ale

(sh) (wh)

fi ____

(sh) (wh)

112   *Week-by-Week Phonics Packets* © 2010 by Joan Novelli and Holly Grundon. Scholastic Teaching Resources

Missing Letters

Look at the picture. Fill in the missing letters. Use the Letter Bank. Read the sentence.

Letter Bank

wh   sh

My ____ell

goes with me

____erever

I go!

What's the Word?

Read each clue. Write the answer.
Use the Word Bank.

Word Bank

push   shout   shower   whale   why

1. Has the little word *how*: _____

2. Does not have *a, e, i, o,* or *u*: _____

3. Has long *a*, like : _____

4. Opposite of *pull*: _____

5. To use a loud voice: _____

Challenge Word

Fill in the missing letters.
Read the word.

Use these letters:

h   s   t

f l a ___ ___ l i g h ___

Make New Words

Fill in **sh** or **wh** to make words.

1. _____ut

2. _____en

3. lea_____

4. _____ite

Circle the word that names the picture.

Name _____ Date _____

Fill-In Story

Look at the Word Bank. Use the words to fill in the blanks. Then read the story!

Word Bank

shadow   shapes   short   what   when

A Shadow Story

Shadows can be tall.

Shadows can be _____.

Shadows come in many _____ and sizes.

_____ makes a shadow? We see a

shadow _____ something blocks light.

When you play outside, your body blocks the

sun's light. This makes a _____

that looks like you!

Word Tree

Think of words with *sh* and *wh*. Write them.

Words With
sh and **wh**

1.

   ○ wheel

   ○ water

2.

   ○ shoe

   ○ shirt

3.

   ○ watch

   ○ whistle

How Did You Do?

How many stars do you give your work?
Color them.

Name _____ Date _____

Words to Know

Sometimes two letters make one sound together.
The letters *c* and *h* go together in chair .
Say the name for each picture. Listen for the
sounds of *ch* and *th*. Underline *ch* and *th*.

bran<u>ch</u>

chair

inch

thirty

thumb

tooth

Word Sort

Look at the words above. Write them in the boxes.

Words With *ch*	Words With *th*
_____	_____
_____	_____
_____	_____

My Checklist

✔ **Check each activity when you complete it.**

Page 1

_____ Words to Know

_____ Word Sort

Page 2

_____ Let's Count!

_____ Missing Letters

Page 3

_____ What's the Word?

_____ Make New Words

_____ Challenge Word

Page 4

_____ Fill–In Story

_____ What Am I?

_____ Extra!

Page 5

_____ Review

Name _____ Date _____

Let's Count!

What can you count? Look at the picture in each box. Choose the missing letters. Write them in the blanks. Read the words.

one loose too____

ch · th

____irty days

ch · th

four legs on a ____air

ch · th

12 in____es in a foot

ch · th

Look at the picture. Fill in the missing letters. Use the Letter Bank. Read the sentence.

Letter Bank

th · ch

This ____ipmunk

is ____inking

about dinner!

Name _____ Date _____

What's the Word?

Read each clue. Write the answer.
Use the Word Bank.

Word Bank

chat   cheek   inch   thin   this

1. Has the little word *is*: _____

2. The opposite of *thick*: _____

3. The letters in this word spell *chin*: _____

4. Another way to say *talk*: _____

5. Part of your face: _____

Make New Words

Fill in **ch** or **th**
to make words.

1. lun_____

2. _____ild

3. ba_____

4. _____en

Circle the word
that names the
picture.

Challenge Word

Fill in the missing letters.
Read the word.

Use these letters:
f   h   t

___ e a ___ ___ e r

Name _____ Date _____

Fill-In Story

Look at the Word Bank. Use the words to fill in the blanks. Then read the story!

Word Bank

cheeks   chipmunk   mouth   their   things

Big Cheek Chipmunk

Chipmunks have big _____!

They use _____ cheeks to

hold food. Chipmunks like to eat

seeds and berries. They like to eat

other _____, too. A _____

can hold lots of food in its _____.

What do you know about chipmunks?

What Am I?

I chomp and I chew.

I mash and grind, too.

What am I?

Answer: ___ ___ ___ ___

Use these letters:
t h t e e

Extra!

Look at the Word Bank. Find the words. Write them.

1. A word with the little word **in**:

   _____

2. A word with the little word **out**:

   _____

Name _____ Date _____

Bubble Time

Say the name for each picture. Fill in the ○ to spell the word. Write the letters in the blank.

1.

   _____ u m b   ○ ch
                   ○ th

2.

   _____ a i r   ○ ch
                   ○ th

3.

   ba _____   ○ ch
                   ○ th

4.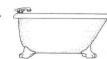

   ear _____   ○ ch
                   ○ th

5.

   bran _____   ○ ch
                   ○ th

How Did You Do?

How many stars do you give your work? Color them.

Name _____ Date _____

Words to Know

The letter *c* has two sounds. A soft *c* sounds like the *c* in *cent* . A hard *c* sounds like the *c* in *cart* . Listen to the sound of *c*. Underline the *c* in each word.

car

cat

celery

city

corn

juice

Word Sort

Look at the words above. Write them in the boxes.

Soft C

_____

_____

_____

Hard C

_____

_____

_____

My Checklist

✔ **Check each activity when you complete it.**

Page 1

_____ Words to Know

_____ Word Sort

Page 2

_____ The C Shop

_____ Missing Letters

Page 3

_____ Puzzle Play

_____ Thumbs Up!

_____ Challenge Word

Page 4

_____ Fill–In Story

_____ What Doesn't Belong?

_____ What Am I?

Page 5

_____ Review

Name _____ Date _____

The C Shop

What does the C Shop sell?
Here's a clue: Everything has
a c in its name. Say the name
for the pictures in each box.
Color the picture that has the
letter c.

Missing Letters

Look at each picture. Fill in the letter **c** to spell each word. Read the sentences.

___at likes

___orn.

___entipede

likes ___ereal.

Week-by-Week Phonics Packets © 2010 by Joan Novelli and Holly Grundon. Scholastic Teaching Resources

Name _____ Date _____

Puzzle Play

Look at each picture. Say the word.
Draw a line to connect the puzzle pieces.

1. | ci | | cil |

2. | pen | | ty |

3. | cook | | corn |

4. | pop | | ies |

Challenge Word

Fill in the missing letters.
Read the word.

This tricky word
has both *c* sounds.
Use these letters:
c m c

i __ e __ r e a __

Thumbs Up!

Say the name
for each picture.
Color 👍 if the
word begins with
c. Color 👎 if it
does not.

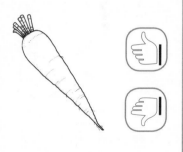

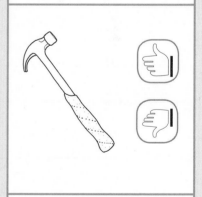

Name _____ Date _____

Fill-In Story

Look at the Word Bank. Use the words to fill in the blanks. Read the story!

Word Bank

carrots   Cat   celery   cookies

Centipede's Garden

"Let's plant a garden," said Centipede.

"What can we grow?" asked _____.

"We can grow _____," said Centipede.

"We can grow _____, too."

"Can we grow _____?" asked Cat.

"No," said Centipede. "Cookies do not

grow in a garden!"

What Am I?

Use these letters:

C   S   C

I dress in old clothes.

I keep away crows.

What am I?

Answer: a ___ ___ are ___ row

What Doesn't Belong?

Look at each picture. Say the words. **X** the word that does not belong.

can   cup

car   corn

cake   cat

Name _____ Date _____

Word Tree

Think of words with c. Write them.

Words With

c

How many stars do you give your work?
Color them.

Extra!

Add the letter **c** to each word. Read your new words.

all + c =

__all

old + c =

__old

an + c =

__an

Name _____ Date _____

Words to Know

The letter *g* has two sounds. A soft *g* sounds like the *g* in *giraffe* . A hard *g* sounds like the *g* in *goat* . Listen to the sound of *g*. Underline the *g* in each word.

cage

flag

gate

giraffe

guitar

orange

Word Sort

Look at the words above. Write them in the boxes.

Soft **g**	Hard **g**
_____	_____
_____	_____
_____	_____

Animal House

Who lives in this house? Here's a clue: Everyone's name has the letter *g*. Say the name for the animal in each box. Circle the word, then write it.

fish   goat

_____

gorilla   dog

_____

penguin   zebra

_____

fox   giraffe

_____

Week-by-Week Phonics Packets © 2010 by Joan Novelli and Holly Grundon. Scholastic Teaching Resources

127

Missing Letters

Look at the picture. Fill in the missing letters. Use the Letter Bank. Read the sentence.

Letter Bank

g   r   g

A hed___eho___

___olls into a ball

to stay safe!

Name _____ Date _____

Puzzle Play

Say the name for each picture. Say the word. Draw a line to connect the puzzle pieces.

1.  ti   fish

2.  gold   ger

3.  gir   gic

4. ma   affe

Challenge Word

Fill in the missing letters. Read the word.

Use these letters:
g   h   g

G e o r ___ e   W a s ___ i n ___ t o n

Thumbs Up!

Say the name for each picture. Color 👍 if the word begins with **g**. Color 👎 if it does not.

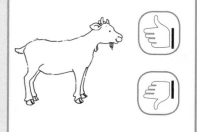

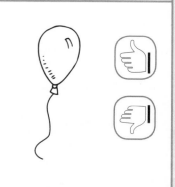

Week-by-Week Phonics Packets © 2010 by Joan Novelli and Holly Grundon. Scholastic Teaching Resources

Name _____ Date _____

Fill-In Story

Look at the Word Bank. Use the words to fill in the blanks. Read the story!

Word Bank

Giraffe

Goldfish

Grasshopper

gumdrops

Who Can Help Goat?

Once upon a time, there was a Gumdrop Tree.

"Who can help me pick the _____?"

asked Goat.

"I can't hop that high," said _____.

"I can't leave the water," said _____.

"I can help you, Goat," said _____.

"My long neck helps me pick leaves from tall trees.

I can pick the gumdrops!"

Say the name for each picture. **X** the pictures that do not end with the sound of *g*.

Name _____ Date _____

Word Tree

Think of words with g. Write them.

Words With
g

Add the letter **g** to each word. Read your new words.

row + g =

___row

ate + g =

___ate

low + g =

___low

How Did You Do?

How many stars do you give your work?
Color them.

Name _____ Date _____

Words to Know

Rhyming words have the same ending sound.
Look at the pictures in each box. Say the words.
Listen to the ending sounds.

fan   van

duck   truck

string   swing

pen   ten

hop   stop

Word Sort

Look at the words above. Write them in the boxes.

Words With 3 Letters	Words With 4 or More Letters
_____	_____
_____	_____
_____	_____
_____	_____
_____	_____

Name _____ Date _____

Frog Hop

Help Frog hop across the pond. Look at the picture in each box. Read the words. Color the lilypad with the rhyming word.

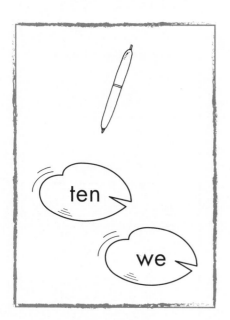

ten

we

and

sing

bug

stop

cup

ran

Name _____ Date _____

Make New Words

Say the name for each picture. Read the word. Use the Letter Bank to make new words. You can use letters more than once.

Letter Bank

bl fl g h l pl s th

clock

_____ ock

_____ ock

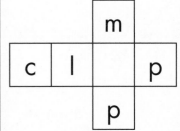

drum

_____ um

_____ um

cat

_____ at

_____ at

ship

_____ ip

_____ ip

Challenge Word

Fill in the missing letters. Read the word.

Use these letters:
c k a

b ___ c k p a ___ ___

Two-Way Words

Fill in the letter that spells a word each way. Use the Letter Bank.

Letter Bank

a o i

	m	
c	l		p
	p	

	w		
f		s	h
	s		
	h		

	h		
s	t		p
	p		

Name _____ Date _____

Fill-In Rhyme

Look at the Word Bank. Use the words to fill in the blanks. Then read the rhyme!

Word Bank

hug   sock   swing

Have You Ever?

Have you ever seen a bug

give someone a _____?

Have you ever seen a king

playing on a _____?

Have you ever seen a clock

that looked like a _____?

I'll take a little guess.

The answer's **NO**, not *yes*!

What Am I?

I am the sound of a clock.

I am not *tick*.

I am ____ ____ ____ ____

Use these letters:
k o t c

Name _____ Date _____

Bubble Time

Look at the picture. Say the word. Fill in the ○ for the word that has the same ending sound.

1.  ○ flat
   ○ can

2.   ○ pat
   ○ then

3.   ○ sit
   ○ fix

4.   ○ hot
   ○ now

5.   ○ did
   ○ hum

How Did You Do?

How many stars do you give your work? Color them.

Buddy Words

Fill in the missing letters to spell rhyming buddy words. Use the Letter Bank.

Letter Bank

wh   br

swing   ____ing

then   ____en

Name _____ Date _____

Words to Know

Rhyming words have the same ending sound.
Look at the pictures in each box. Say the words.
Listen to the ending sounds.

pail   snail

flies   ties

sheep   jeep

bow   crow

Word Sort

Look at the words above. Write them in the boxes.

Long *a* and Long *e* ending	Long *i* and Long *o* ending
_____	_____
_____	_____
_____	_____
_____	_____

My Checklist

✔ Check each activity when you complete it.

Page 1

_____ Words to Know

_____ Word Sort

Page 2

_____ Down the Slide

_____ Missing Letters

Page 3

_____ What's the Word?

_____ Make New Words

_____ Challenge Word

Page 4

_____ Fill–In Story

_____ What Doesn't Belong?

_____ Missing Letters

Page 5

_____ Review

Name _____ Date _____

Down the Slide

Help the animals go down the slides! Say the
name for each animal. Circle the rhyming word.

pail

take

snow

shop

feet

sleep

mail

nice

mine

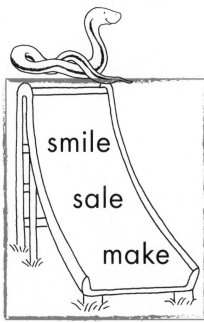

smile

sale

make

Missing Letters

Look at the
picture. Fill in the
missing letters.
Use the Letter
Bank. Read the
sentence.

Letter Bank

o w c r

Can a

___ ___ow

r___ ___ a

boat? No!

Name _____ Date _____

What's the Word?

Read each clue. Use the Word Bank to find the answers.

Word Bank

crow   nail   rice   three

1. Part of a finger or toe that rhymes with 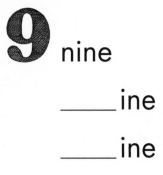 :

_____

2. An animal that rhymes with :

_____

3. A food that rhymes with :

_____

4. A number word that rhymes with :

_____

Challenge Word

Fill in the missing letters. Read the word.

Use these letters:
i h g

n i g h t l ___ ___ ___ t

Make New Words

Look at each picture. Read the word. Fill in the blanks to make new rhyming words. Use the Letter Bank.

Letter Bank

cl   f   m   th

9 nine

____ine

____ine

rose

____ose

____ose

Name _____ Date _____

Fill-In Story

Look at the Word Bank. Use the words to fill in the blanks with rhyming words. Read the story!

Word Bank

tie   throne   jeep   rake   snail

A Whale of a Sale

"What a big sale!" said Whale.

"Will I buy a **cake** or a new _____?"

"Will I buy a **pie** or a bow _____?"

"Will I buy a _____ that goes **beep**?"

"Will I buy a **phone** or a big _____?"

"No," said Whale. "I will buy a **pail** for

my friend _____!"

Missing Letters

What is another title for the story?
Fill in the missing letters.

Use these letters:
e l a

A Whale T____ ____ ____

Say the name for each picture. **X** the pictures that do not sound like .

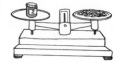

Name _____ Date _____

Bubble Time

Say the name for each picture. Fill in the ○ for the word that has the same ending sound.

1.    ○ late
   ○ five

2.    ○ knot
   ○ keep

3.   ○ grow
   ○ ride

4.    ○ slow
   ○ have

5.   ○ sleep
   ○ three

How Did You Do?

How many stars do you give your work?
Color them.

Make New Words

Look at each picture. Read the word. Use letters from the Letter Bank to make words. Write your words.

Letter Bank
n t m d

cake

1. ____ake

   ____ake

mice

2. ____ice

   ____ice

Name _____ Date _____

Words to Know

Rhyming words have the same ending sound.
Look at the pictures in each box. Say the words.
Listen to the ending sounds.

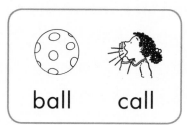

ball   call

clown   crown

moon   spoon

mouse   house

Word Sort

Look at the words above. Write them in the boxes.

Double-Letter Words	Other Words

House of Rhymes

Which words live in this house? Say the name for each picture. Circle the word ending. Fill in the blanks to spell rhyming words.

-ouse   -oot

m_____   h_____

-oot   -ook

b_____   l_____

-aw   -own

cl_____   d_____

-oon   -oud

sp_____   s_____

Name _____ Date _____

Buddy Words

Look at the picture in each box. Read the word. Fill in the missing letter to spell a rhyming word. Use the Letter Bank.

Letter Bank

t z

book   ___ook

broom   ___oom

Challenge Word

Fill in the missing letters. Read the word.

Use these letters:

o k o b

c ___ ___ k ___ o o ___

Make New Words

Look at each picture. Read the word. Use letters from the Letter Bank to make words. Write your words.

Letter Bank

d h p t

crown

1. ___own

___own

chair

2. ___air

___air

Riddle Time

Read the riddles. Fill in the missing letters.
Use the Letter Bank.

Letter Bank

c l n t

1. I rhyme with **cloud** .

   I am not quiet,

   I am ____oud.

2. I rhyme with **moon** .

   I am not morning,

   I am ____oon.

3. I rhyme with **ball** .

   I am not short

   I am ____all.

4. I rhyme with **school** .

   I am not warm

   I am ____ool.

Name _____ Date _____

Bubble Time

Say the name for each picture. Look at the beginning letters. Fill in the ○ to spell the words. Write the letters in the blank.

1. h_____ and m_____   ○ ouse

                                ○ oud

2. b_____ and t_____   ○ oud

                                ○ ook

3. cl_____ and br_____   ○ ool

                                ○ own

4. m_____ and s_____   ○ oon

                                ○ ool

How Did You Do?

How many stars do you give your work?
Color them. ☆ ☆ ☆ ☆ ☆

Week-by-Week Phonics Packets © 2010 by Joan Novelli and Holly Grundon. Scholastic Teaching Resources

Extra!

Look at the picture. Read the word. Fill in the blanks to spell three words that rhyme with *ball*.

ball

_____all

_____all

_____all

145

Name _____ Date _____

Words to Know

Words can have 1 syllable, like *car* .
Words can have 2 syllables, like *apple* .
Words can have more syllables. Say the name
for each picture. Clap and count the syllables.

apple

bird

car

elephant

flower

umbrella

Word Sort

Look at the words above. Write them in the boxes.

1 Syllable

_____   _____

2 Syllables

_____   _____

3 Syllables

_____   _____

Name _____ Date _____

I Spy Animals

Play I Spy Animals. Say the name for the animals in each box. Clap and count the syllables for each. Color the animal that matches the number of syllables.

Say the name for each picture. Fill in the missing letters. Use the Letter Bank.

2	1

3	2

Letter Bank

der   tle

I am a
tur_____.

I am a
spi_____.

Name _____ Date _____

Make New Words

Use a word part from each box to make words.
Write your words.

Beginning		
pud	hap	
tur	go	
num	my	

End		
py	ber	
self	tle	
ing	dle	

<u>happy</u>

_____

_____

_____

_____

_____

Challenge Word

Fill in the missing letters.
Read the word.

Use these letters:
t l p

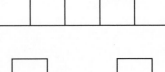

c a __ e r __ i __ l a r

Shape Match

Look at each word. Find the matching shape. Write the letters in the boxes. Read the words.

book   baby

radio

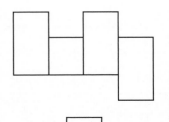

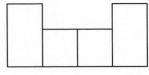

Riddle Time

Read the riddles. Write the answers. Use the
Word Bank. Clap the syllables for each.

Word Bank

apple   barn   tiger   umbrella

1. I have two *p*'s.

   I grow on trees.

   What am I?

   Answer: an _____

2. I have a long *i*

   And I say *grrrrrr*!

   What am I?

   Answer: a _____

3. I don't sing *do, re, mi, fa, so*

   But at the end I say *la*.

   What am I?

   Answer: an _____

4. Clap and count just 1,

   Then this word is done.

   What am I?

   Answer: a _____

Extra!

Look at the Word
Bank. Write the
words to tell how
many syllables.

1 syllable

_____

2 syllables

_____

_____

3 syllables

_____

Bubble Time

Look at each picture. Say the word. Fill in the ○ that tells how many syllables.

1. bee
   ○ 1
   ○ 2
   ○ 3

2. pretzel
   ○ 1
   ○ 2
   ○ 3

3. ruler
   ○ 1
   ○ 2
   ○ 3

4. strawberry
   ○ 1
   ○ 2
   ○ 3

5. ring
   ○ 1
   ○ 2
   ○ 3

6. elephant
   ○ 1
   ○ 2
   ○ 3

How Did You Do?

How many stars do you give your work?
Color them.

What Doesn't Belong?

Say the name for each picture. **X** the picture in each row that does not match the number of syllables.

1

2

3

Words to Know

A compound word is a word that is made up of two smaller words: **cup + cake = cupcake**. Read each small word. Read the compound words.

(air) + (plane)

airplane

(back) + (pack)

backpack

(foot) + (print)

footprint

(inch) + (worm)

inchworm

(pop) + (corn)

popcorn

(up) + (stairs)

upstairs

Word Sort

Look at the words above. Write them in the boxes.

Begins With a Vowel	Begins With a Consonant
_____	_____
_____	_____
_____	_____

Time for School

Look at each picture. Put the words together to spell a compound word. Use the words to tell a story about school.

back + pack

_____

lunch + box

_____

note + book

_____

class + room

_____

Missing Letters

Look at the picture. Fill in the missing letters. Use the Letter Bank. Read the sentence.

Letter Bank

k   t   w

"Did you

ea___ my

home___or___?"

Name _____ Date _____

Puzzle Play

Look at each puzzle piece. Draw a line to make compound words. Write the words.

1.  door   house

2.  dog   bell

3.  cup   bow

4.  rain   cake

Make New Words

Say the name for each picture. Put two words together to spell a compound word. Use the Word Bank.

Word Bank

bug   plane

air + **?** ____

_____

lady + **?** ____

_____

Challenge Word

Look at the picture. Fill in the missing letters to spell a compound word.

Use these letters:
t   d   a

s k ___ ___ e b o a r ___

Name _____ Date _____

Riddle Time

Read the riddles. Fill in the blanks.
Use the Word Bank.

Word Bank

hive hot fire fish

1. I am a star

   But I live in the ocean.

   I am a star_____.

2. I am dog

   But you put me in a bun.

   I am a _____ dog.

3. I am a home for honey

   And I rhyme with .

   I am a bee _____.

4. I light up the night

   But I am not a lamp.

   I am a _____ fly.

Word Tree

Read each word. Put words together to make compound words. You can use words more than once. Write your words on the tree.

pan   foot

ball   base

man   **Compound Words**   cake

snow   cup

_____

_____

_____

_____

_____

How many stars do you give your work? Color them.

   ☆ ☆

Bubble Time

Say the name for each picture. Fill in the ○ to spell the compound word.

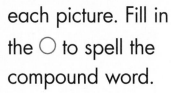 sand_____

○ box

○ fox

 tea_____

○ cap

○ cup

 tug_____

○ bake

○ boat

Name _____ Date _____

Words to Know

Plural means *more than one*. Look at the pictures. Read the words. Underline the plural words.

baby
babies

book
books

box
boxes

bus
buses

cake
cakes

puppy
puppies

Word Sort

Look at the words above. Write the words for *more than one*.

To make this word plural...

Just Add s

_____   _____

Add es

_____   _____

Drop the y and add ies

_____   _____

Name _____ Date _____

Field Trip!

Take a field trip to a farm! Look at the picture in each box. Circle the word, then write it. Tell a story about the field trip.

bus

buses

_____

puppies

puppy

_____

chicks

chick

_____

lamb

lambs

_____

Look at the picture. Fill in the missing letters. Use the Letter Bank. Read the sentence.

Letter Bank

es   s

The kitten__ are asleep in their dish__ __!

Name _____ Date _____

Spelling Scramble

Say the name for each picture.
Unscramble the letters to spell the word.

1. e s k i t   _ _ _ _

2. b t o o s   _ _ _ _ _

3. e s f o x   _ _ _ _ _

4. i e s l f   _ _ _ _ _

Challenge Word

Sometimes the word for more than one has a different spelling. Fill in the letters to spell the word for more than one **child**.

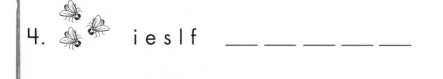

Use these letters:
n e r

c h i l d _ _ _ _

Buddy Words

Fill in the missing letters to make plural words. Use the Letter Bank. Read your words.

Letter Bank

es   ies   s

ball _____

lunch _____

berr _____

Fill-In Rhyme

Fill in the blanks. Read the poem with a friend.

More Than One

More than one **dog** is **dogs.**

And more than one **frog** is _____.

More than one **box** is **boxes**

And more than one **fox** is _____.

More than one **cherry** is **cherries**.

And more than one **berry** is _____.

More than one **goose** is **geese**.

But more than one **moose** is NOT **meese!**

(It's just moose!)

Extra!

Some words for one and more than one are the same. Look at the pictures. Write the words.

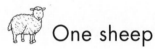 One sheep

Two _____

 One moose

Two _____

Bubble Time

Say the word for each picture.
Fill in the ○ for that word.

1.
   - ○ girls
   - ○ read
   - ○ girl

2.
   - ○ watch
   - ○ inches
   - ○ watches

3.
   - ○ boy
   - ○ yard
   - ○ boys

4.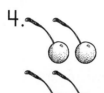
   - ○ chair
   - ○ cherries
   - ○ inches

5.
   - ○ bus
   - ○ buses
   - ○ boots

6.
   - ○ inches
   - ○ chip
   - ○ inch

How Did You Do?

How many stars do you give your work?
Color them. ☆ ☆ ☆ ☆ ☆

What Doesn't Belong?

Look at each picture. **X** the word that does not name the picture.

bird   birds

babies   baby

dish   dishes